Noah's Science Adventures:

On the Trail of Amazing Discoveries

Written By: Alisa L. Grace

Illustrated By: naqsa_art

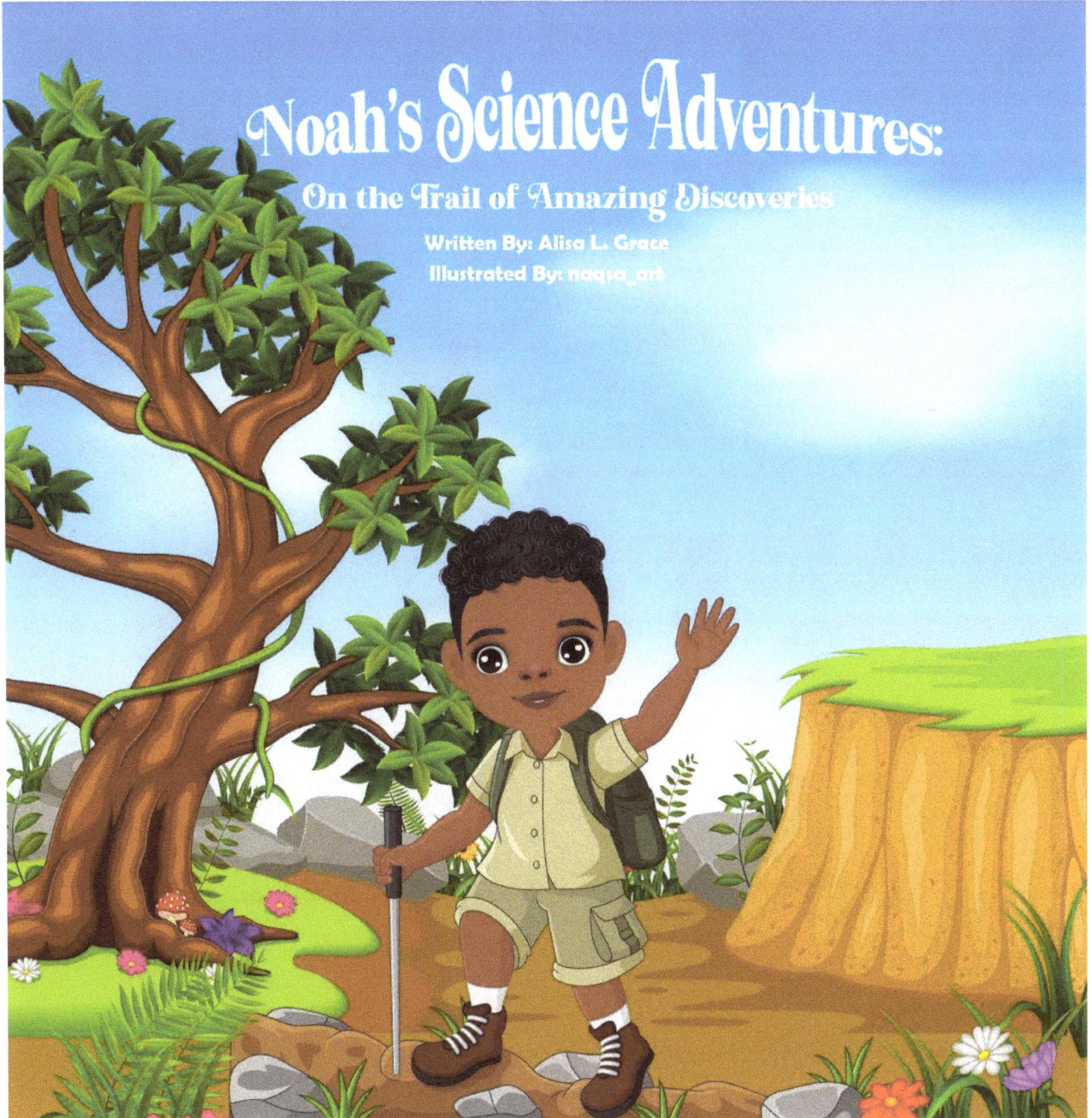

Noah's Science Adventures:
On the Trail of Amazing Discoveries

Written by
Alisa L. Grace

Self-Published by
Alisa L. Grace
Sanford, FL 32771

ISBN: 978-1-966129-17-2

First Edition

Printed in the United States of America

Library of Congress Cataloging-in-Publication Data
Grace, Alisa L.
Title of the Book: Noah's Science Adventures: On the Trail of Amazing Discoveries
Library of Congress Control Number: 2024923781

Disclaimer: The views expressed in this book are those of the author and do not necessarily reflect any organizations or individuals mentioned.

Acknowledgments: The author wishes to thank God, Her Husband (Linion), Victory Temple of God, Florida SPECS, Unity Youth Association, All About Serving You, Angels-ANJ Events, NordeVest, and Love & Create Life for their support and contributions.

This book is dedicated To our precious Noah,

May your curiosity and sense of wonder never end. May this book ignite a passion to pursue incredible discoveries in the world around you. May your exploration of God's creation fill you with awe and amazement. May this book remind you of your insatiable curiosity and love for learning. We are incredibly proud of the remarkable scientist you are becoming!

Love always,
NeNe

Welcome to
"Noah's Science Adventures"!

Hey Noah,

Get ready to blast off on a fantastic adventure! This book guides you to explore the world around you like a real scientist. You have your super cool video camcorder, extraordinary brain, and love for asking "Why?"—that's all you need!

But first, let's talk about a secret weapon you have: your "inferencing" powers! It's like having a superpower that enables you to be a detective and figure things out using clues. Just like when you see steam rising from your food, you can infer it's hot! Dad is putting on his uniform; you can infer he is going to work on the military base.

This book is jam-packed with exciting adventures where you'll use your inferencing skills to uncover the mysteries of science. You'll be tracking amazing ants on the playground, watching the clouds dance in the sky, digging into dinosaur secrets at the museum, meeting incredible animals at the zoo, and exploring nature trails like a true explorer.

Here's a sneak peek at the awesome things you'll be doing:

- **Chapter 1: The Amazing Ant Trails:** Get ready to follow those busy ants and figure out where they're going and what they're up to!
- **Chapter 2: The Mystery of the Moving Clouds:** You'll become a cloud detective and discover why clouds move and change shape.
- **Chapter 3: The Dinosaur Detectives:** Travel back in time to uncover clues about dinosaurs and their lives.
- **Chapter 4: Animal Adventures at the Zoo:** Get ready to meet amazing animals worldwide and learn how they survive in their habitats.
- **Chapter 5: Nature Trail Explorers:** Put on your explorer hat and discover the secrets hidden in nature, from animal tracks to incredible plants.

Remember Noah; The Bible tells us that God created everything around us, and we can learn so much about Him by exploring His creation. So grab your camcorder, put on your scientist hat, and prepare for an adventure you'll never forget!

Table of Contents

Introduction

Get ready to put on your explorer hat and grab your video camcorder because "Noah's Science Adventures: On the Trail of Amazing Discoveries" is about to begin!

This book is about YOU, Noah – a super curious kid who loves to ask "why?" You're a scientist in the making, always observing, always wondering, and always ready to discover something new. And guess what? You have your own special tool to help you on your quests: your trusty video camcorder!

In this book, you'll join your awesome family—your dad, who's always up for an adventure (especially since he's in the military!); your mom, who helps you understand the amazing things you see; and your playful little sister, Kenlyn, who makes everything more fun.

Together, you'll be going on exciting expeditions, like:

- **Unraveling the mystery of the amazing ant trails** right on your military base playground.
- **Becoming a cloud detective** to figure out how those fluffy shapes move and change in the sky.
- **Traveling back in time** to the museum to uncover dinosaur secrets hidden in ancient fossils.
- **Going on a wild safari** at the zoo to meet incredible animals from all over the world.
- **Transforming into a nature explorer** to find hidden treasures and unique creatures on exciting nature trails.

But here's the secret ingredient to your amazing discoveries: your "inferencing" powers! It's like having a detective's magnifying glass for your brain! Inferencing means using clues to figure things out, just like when you see smoke, you know there's a fire somewhere.

So, get ready to power up your camcorder, put on your thinking cap, and open your eyes to the wonders all around you. "Noah's Science Adventures: On the Trail of Amazing Discoveries" will take you on a journey you'll never forget!

Proverbs 6:6-8 states: "Take a lesson from the ants, you lazybones. Learn from their ways and become wise! Though they have no prince or governor or ruler to make them work, they labor hard all summer, gathering food for the winter."

Chapter 1
The Ant Obstacle Course Challenge (On Base)

The morning sun was shining bright on the military base playground. Noah, with his trusty video camcorder in hand, was ready for an adventure! He loved exploring, and today was no different. As he zoomed around the playground, something caught his eye – a long, wiggly line of tiny creatures marching across the blacktop.

"Whoa, cool!" Noah exclaimed, switching on his camcorder. "Look at all those ants!" He zoomed in, getting a close-up of the ants carrying crumbs and other exciting things. "They look like tiny little construction workers!"

He remembered what "inferencing" meant – it was like being a detective and using clues to figure things out. "Hmm," Noah pondered, "where do you think they're going with all that stuff?" He pointed the camcorder at himself. "I think they're taking the food back to their home. Maybe it's a giant anthill somewhere under the playground!"

Just then, Dad walked over. "Whatcha filming, Noah?" he asked.

"Ants!" Noah said excitedly. "But I don't know where they're going."

"Well, how about we help them... or maybe make it a little harder for them?" Dad winked. Together, they gathered some small twigs, leaves, and pebbles to make a mini obstacle course for the ants.

"Whoa, look!" Noah shouted as he filmed the ants. "They're going over the twigs! And they're working together to move that big crumb over the leaves!"

Mom came over with Kenlyn, who was giggling at the ants. "That's teamwork!" Mom said. "Just like when you and Kenlyn work together to clean up your toys."

"Why do they work together like that?" Noah wondered.

Mom smiled. "That's a great question! Why do you think they do?"

Noah thought for a moment, observing the ants. "Maybe they can't carry the food alone?" he inferred.

"That's a great inference, Noah!" Mom said. "They work together to achieve a common goal." She pointed to a crumb. "What do you think would happen if we moved this crumb?"

"Hmm," Noah pondered, zooming his camera in on the crumb. "Maybe they would get confused and have to find it again?"

"Let's try it and see!" Kenlyn squealed.

Dad carefully moved the crumb a few inches to the side. After a moment of confusion, the ants followed the scent trail to the new location and continued their march.

"Wow!" Noah exclaimed, recording the whole thing. "They're like a tiny army! They never give up!"

Later that day, Noah and Dad looked up ants in his science book and even found a verse in the Bible about them! Proverbs 6:6-8 said, "Go to the ant, you sluggard; consider its ways and be wise! It has no commander, no overseer or ruler, yet it stores its provisions in summer and gathers its food at harvest."

Noah learned that ants are super strong and work together to gather food for their whole colony. He was amazed by how such tiny creatures could be so intelligent and organized. It was a day of amazing discoveries, and it all started with a simple observation and some awesome inferencing!

Activity:
The Amazing Ant Obstacle Course

Objective: To observe ant behavior, practice inferencing skills, and learn about teamwork and communication in an ant colony.

Materials:

- Noah's video camcorder
- Small objects to create an obstacle course (twigs, leaves, pebbles, small blocks, etc.)
- Magnifying glass (optional)
- Notebook and pencil (optional)
- Snacks or crumbs for the ants (optional)

Procedure:

1. **Find the Ants:** Head to the playground and look for a line of ants. Where are they going? What are they carrying?

2. **Record and Predict:** Zoom in on the camcorder and record the ants. Have Noah narrate his observations and predict where the ants are going and what they are doing.

3. **Build an Obstacle Course:** Work together as a family to create a miniature obstacle course for the ants. Use the materials to make bridges, tunnels, or barriers in the ants' path.

4. **Observe and Infer:** Observe how the ants react to the obstacles. Do they go over, under, or around them? Do they work together to overcome the challenges? Record the ants' behavior with the camcorder.

5. **Ask Questions:** Encourage Noah to question and make inferences about the ants' behavior. Mom can ask open-ended questions to guide his thinking:

   - "Why do you think the ants are following each other?"
   - "How do they know where to go?"
   - "What would happen if we moved one of the obstacles?"
   - "How do the ants communicate with each other?"

6. **Experiment:** Try different obstacles to see how the ants respond. What happens if you make the obstacle course more challenging?

7. **Research and Reflect:** Look up information about ants in books or online. Learn about different types of ants and their roles in a colony. Discuss the importance of teamwork and communication for ants and people.

8. **Scripture Connection:** Read Proverbs 6:6-8 together and discuss how the ants demonstrate wisdom and preparedness.

Tips for Parents:

- Encourage Noah to take the lead in observing and recording the ants.
- Ask open-ended questions to stimulate his thinking and help him make inferences.
- Help him connect his observations to the science concepts of insect behavior, communication, and teamwork.
- Relate the activity to the scripture verse and discuss the importance of learning from nature.
- Most importantly, have fun exploring the amazing world of ants together!

He covers the sky with clouds;he supplies the earth with rain and makes grass grow on the hills.
Psalm 147:8

Do you know how the clouds hang poised, those wonders of him who has perfect knowledge?

Job 37:16

Chapter 2
The Cloud Puzzle

Noah loved sunny days, but today was extra special. It wasn't just sunny; the sky was filled with puffy white clouds that looked like cotton candy! He grabbed his camcorder and raced into the backyard.

"Look at those clouds!" he shouted, pointing towards the sky.

Mom sipped iced tea on the patio, and Dad pushed Kenlyn on the swing. "They look like giant marshmallows!" Kenlyn giggled.

"They're amazing," Noah agreed. He set up his camcorder on the picnic table, pointing it towards the sky. "I'm going to make a time-lapse video!" He'd learned how to do that last week, and it made even slow things look super fast.

Noah lay back on the grass as the camcorder whirred, watching the clouds drift by. "Why do they move, Mom?" he asked.

"That's because of the wind, Noah," Mom explained. "The wind pushes the clouds across the sky."

"Like when I blow on a dandelion?" Noah asked, remembering how the seeds flew away.

"Exactly!" Mom smiled.

Dad joined them, pointing upwards. "See that fluffy one that looks like a sheep? That's a cumulus cloud. They usually mean good weather."

Noah zoomed in with his camcorder. "And those wispy ones?"

"Those are cirrus clouds," Dad said. "They're way up high, made of ice crystals. Sometimes, they mean rain is coming."

Noah watched as the clouds changed shape, morphing from dragons to dinosaurs to giant cotton balls. He wondered what kind of weather they might bring. He knew inferencing meant using clues to figure things out, just like he did with the ants.

"Hmm," he thought, "those dark gray clouds over there look kind of heavy. Maybe they'll bring rain?"

A gentle breeze picked up, and the clouds started moving faster. The dark gray ones were getting closer!

"Looks like you might be right, Noah!" Dad said, looking at the sky. We should head inside soon.

Noah quickly packed up his camcorder. He couldn't wait to watch the time-lapse video and see how the clouds danced across the sky.

Inside, Mom opened her Bible and showed Noah a verse in Psalm 147:8: "He covers the sky with clouds; he supplies the earth with rain and makes grass grow on the hills."

"Wow," Noah said, "God made the clouds!"

Mom nodded. "And Job 37:16 talks about how amazing the clouds are, hanging in the sky."

Noah thought about how the clouds brought rain to water the plants and make everything grow. He realized that even something as simple as a cloud was a wonder of God's creation. He couldn't wait to learn more about the weather and all the fantastic things in the world around him.

Activity:
Cloud Gazing and Weather Forecasting

Objective: To observe different cloud types, practice inferencing skills, and learn about weather patterns.

Materials:

- Noah's video camcorder
- Blankets or chairs for comfortable cloud gazing
- Notebook and colored pencils
- Cloud identification chart (optional)

Procedure:

1. **Find a Spot:** Choose a comfortable spot in the backyard or on the base with a clear view of the sky.

2. **Observe and Record:** Lie back and observe the clouds. What shapes do you see? How are they moving? Use the camcorder to record the clouds and create a time-lapse video.

3. **Identify Cloud Types:** Identify different types of clouds (cumulus, cirrus, stratus). Use a cloud identification chart if you have one.

4. **Make Inferences:** Encourage Noah to make inferences about the weather based on the clouds.

   - "What kind of weather do you think those clouds might bring?"
   - "Why do you think the clouds are moving in that direction?"
   - "How do the clouds change over time?"

5. Draw and Describe: Draw pictures of the different cloud types you observe. Write descriptions of the clouds and the weather they might bring.

6. Scripture Connection: Read Psalm 147:8 and Job 37:16 together. Discuss how God created the clouds and how they are a part of His plan for the earth.

Tips for Parents:

- Encourage Noah to use his imagination and creativity while observing the clouds.
- Help him connect his observations to the science concepts of wind, weather patterns, and cloud formation.
- Discuss the importance of observing the world around us and making inferences based on what we see.
- Enjoy the peaceful experience of cloud gazing together and appreciate the beauty of God's creation.

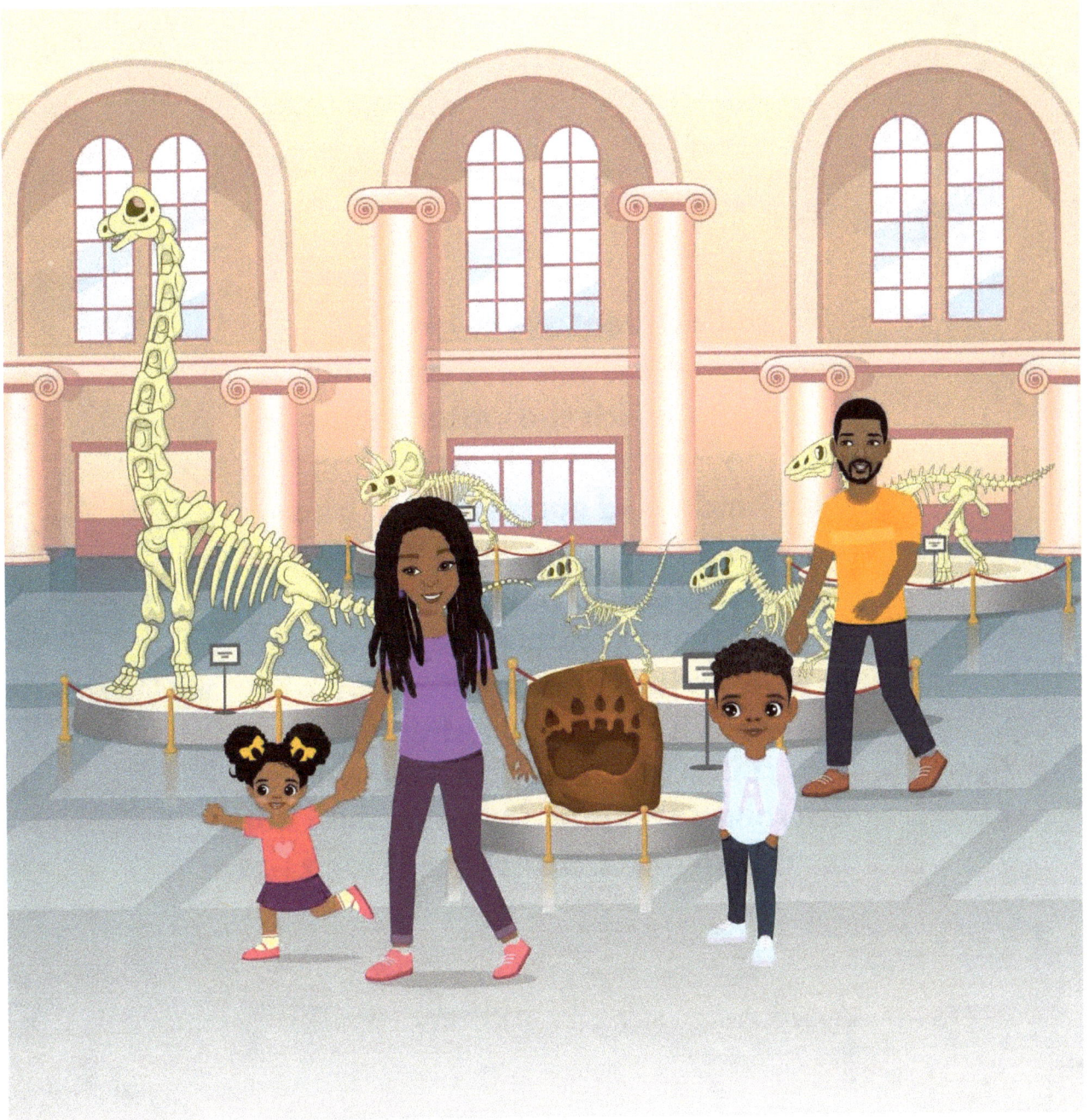

So God created the great
creatures of the sea and every living
thing with which the water teems and
that moves about in it, according to
their kinds, and every winged bird
according to its kind. And God saw
that it was good. Genesis 1:21
O Lord, how manifold are thy works!
in wisdom hast thou made them all:
the earth is full of thy riches.
So is this great and wide sea, wherein
are things creeping innumerable, both
small and great beasts. Psalm 104:24-25

Chapter 3
Dinosaur Detectives

The towering skeletons loomed over Noah, their bones casting long shadows in the dim light of the dinosaur exhibit at the NC Museum of Natural Sciences. He felt like he'd stepped into a prehistoric world! He gripped his camcorder, ready to document every amazing detail.

"Wow!" he whispered, pointing the camera at a massive Triceratops skull. "Look at those horns!" He zoomed in on the giant frill and imagined the dinosaur charging through a jungle.

"This one's even bigger!" Dad exclaimed, standing beneath the long neck of a Brachiosaurus. "It must have been taller than our house!"

Noah swung his camcorder around, trying to capture the whole skeleton in one shot. "It's like a giraffe, but way bigger!"

Mom pointed to a display case filled with fossils. "Look, Noah, those are dinosaur footprints!"

Noah peered at the fossilized tracks. "They're huge! I wonder how fast they could run." He imagined a herd of dinosaurs thundering across the land, leaving those giant footprints behind.

He remembered what he'd learned about inferencing. By looking at the clues, he could figure things out about these amazing creatures, even though they lived millions of years ago.

"Hmm," Noah pondered, "those sharp teeth on that Tyrannosaurus Rex... it must have been a meat-eater!" He pretended to be a paleontologist, reporting his findings into the camcorder. "This just in! We have evidence that T-Rex was a fearsome predator!"

Dad read from a nearby plaque: "Tyrannosaurus Rex had a bite force stronger than any other land animal!"

"Whoa!" Noah exclaimed. "That's incredible!"

Mom pointed to a model of a Stegosaurus. "Look at the plates on its back. Why do you think it had those, Noah?"

Noah examined the plates closely. "Maybe for protection?" he inferred. "Like a shield?"

"That's a great inference!" Mom said. "Scientists believe they were used for defense and to regulate body temperature."

Noah continued exploring the exhibit, his camcorder capturing every fascinating fossil and skeleton. He learned about different types of dinosaurs, their habitats, and what they might have eaten. He even learned about how scientists use fossils to piece together the story of these ancient creatures.

But one question lingered in his mind. "Dad, why aren't there dinosaurs anymore?"

Dad explained that scientists believe a catastrophic event, like a giant asteroid, caused the dinosaurs to become extinct.

"That's sad," Noah said.

Mom nodded. "But it's also a reminder of how precious life is." She opened her Bible and showed Noah Genesis 1:21: "So God created the great creatures of the sea and every living thing with which the water teems and that moves about in it, according to their kinds, and every winged bird according to its kind. And God saw that it was good."

"Even the dinosaurs?" Noah asked.

"Yes, even the dinosaurs," Mom confirmed. "God created them, and they were a part of His amazing creation."

They also read Psalm 104:24-25: "How many are your works, Lord! In wisdom, you made them all; the earth is full of your creatures. There is the sea, vast and spacious, teeming with creatures beyond number—living things both large and small."

Noah was filled with wonder. He thought about all the amazing creatures God had created, past and present. He felt like a real dinosaur detective, uncovering clues to the past and learning about God's incredible creation.

Activity:
Fossil Fun!

Objective: To learn about fossils, practice making inferences, and explore the concept of extinction.

Materials:

- Modeling clay or playdough
- Small objects (shells, leaves, plastic dinosaurs, etc.)
- Plaster of Paris (optional)
- Pictures of fossils (optional)

Procedure:

1. **Examine Fossils:** Look at pictures of fossils or, if possible, visit a museum with real fossils. Discuss what fossils are and how they are formed.

2. **Make Fossil Imprints:** Roll out the clay or playdough. Press the small objects into the clay to make imprints.

3. **Create Plaster Fossils (Optional):** If using plaster of Paris, follow the instructions to mix it. Pour the plaster over the clay imprints and let it dry. Carefully remove the clay to reveal the plaster fossils.

4. **Infer and Discuss:** Examine the fossil imprints or plaster fossils.

   o "What can you tell about the object that made this imprint?"
   o "What do you think this creature might have looked like?"
   o "How do you think this fossil was formed?"
   o "What can fossils teach us about the past?"

5. Extinction Discussion: Talk about extinction. Why do some animals disappear? What can we do to protect animals today?

6. Scripture Connection: Read Genesis 1:21 and Psalm 104:24-25. Discuss how God created all creatures and how we can learn about His creation by studying fossils.

Tips for Parents:

- Encourage Noah to use his imagination and creativity while making fossil imprints.
- Help him connect the activity to the science concepts of paleontology, fossils, and extinction.
- Discuss the importance of respecting and protecting God's creation.
- Have fun creating your own "fossil collection" together!

And God made the beasts of the earth according to their kinds and the livestock according to their kinds, and everything that creeps on the ground according to its kind. And God saw that it was good. Genesis 1:25

For every beast of the forest is mine, and the cattle upon a thousand hills. I know all the fowls of the mountains: and the wild beasts of the field are mine. Psalm 50:10-11

Chapter 4
Safari Adventure!

The African savanna stretched out before Noah like a giant, sun-drenched painting. He felt a thrill of excitement as he stepped into the exhibit at the NC Zoo, his camcorder ready to capture the incredible sights and sounds. Giraffes with necks like telephone poles grazed peacefully, zebras with dazzling stripes galloped in the distance, and a pride of lions lounged in the shade.

"Wow!" Noah whispered, zooming in on a graceful gazelle. "It's like being in Africa!"

"Look, Noah!" Dad pointed. "There's a rhinoceros!"

The massive creature lumbered past, its thick skin and powerful horn making it look like a living tank. Noah recorded the rhino with his camcorder, narrating his observations. "The rhino has really thick skin... I bet that protects it from the thorns and branches."

Mom pointed to a group of zebras grazing nearby. "Why do you think zebras have stripes, Noah?" she asked.

Noah thought for a moment, observing the zebras as they moved. "Maybe it helps them hide from predators?" he inferred. "The stripes make it hard to see them in the tall grass."

"That's right!" Mom said. "It's called camouflage."

Dad pointed to a giraffe nibbling leaves from a tall acacia tree. "How does the giraffe reach those leaves, Noah?"

Noah watched as the giraffe stretched its long neck, its tongue wrapping around a branch. "It has a super long neck!" he exclaimed. "It's like a built-in ladder!"

"Exactly!" Dad said. "Giraffes have adapted to reach food that other animals can't."

Noah noticed a group of lions lying in the shade. One lion lifted its head and gazed intently across the savanna. "What do you think the lion is waiting for?" Noah whispered, zooming in with his camcorder.

"Probably its next meal," Dad said. "Lions are predators at the top of the food chain."

Noah learned about how the animals depended on each other, from the tiny insects to the mighty lions. He saw how each animal was perfectly adapted to its environment, with unique features that helped it survive.

As they were leaving the exhibit, Mom opened her Bible and showed Noah Genesis 1:25: "God made the wild animals according to their kinds, the livestock according to their kinds and all the creatures that move along the ground according to their kinds. And God saw that it was good."

"God made all these amazing animals?" Noah asked, his eyes wide with wonder.

Mom nodded. "Every single one."

They also read Psalm 50:10-11: "For every animal of the forest is mine, and the cattle on a thousand hills. I know every bird in the mountains and the insects in the fields are mine."

"Wow," Noah said. "God cares for all the animals, even the lions and the rhinos!"

Noah left the zoo that day with a heart full of awe and a camcorder full of amazing footage. He couldn't wait to learn more about the incredible animals God created and the wonderful world they live in.

Activity:
Animal Adaptations

Objective: To learn about animal adaptations, practice inferencing skills, and explore the concept of food chains.

Materials:

- Pictures of different animals (from books, magazines, or online)
- Paper and pencils or crayons
- Animal fact books or internet access (optional)

Procedure:

1. Observe and Describe: Look at pictures of different animals. Discuss their physical features and behaviors.

2. Infer Adaptations: Encourage Noah to make inferences about how the animals' features help them survive in their habitats.

- o "Why do you think the camel has humps?"
- o "How does the polar bear stay warm in the Arctic?"
- o "Why does the eagle have sharp talons?"

3. Draw and Label: Draw pictures of the animals and label their adaptations. Explain how each adaptation helps the animal survive.

4. Food Chain Fun: Create a simple food chain using the animals you've discussed. For example, grass -> zebra -> lion. Explain how energy flows through the food chain.

5. **Research and Learn:** Choose an animal from the zoo and research its habitat, diet, and adaptations. Create a fact sheet with pictures and information.

6. **Scripture Connection:** Read Genesis 1:25 and Psalm 50:10-11. Discuss how God created all animals with unique characteristics and how He cares for them all.

Tips for Parents:

- Encourage Noah to ask questions and explore the reasons behind animal adaptations.
- Help him connect the activity to the science concepts of habitats, adaptations, and food chains.
- Discuss the importance of respecting and protecting animals and their environments.
- Have fun learning about the amazing diversity of God's creation!

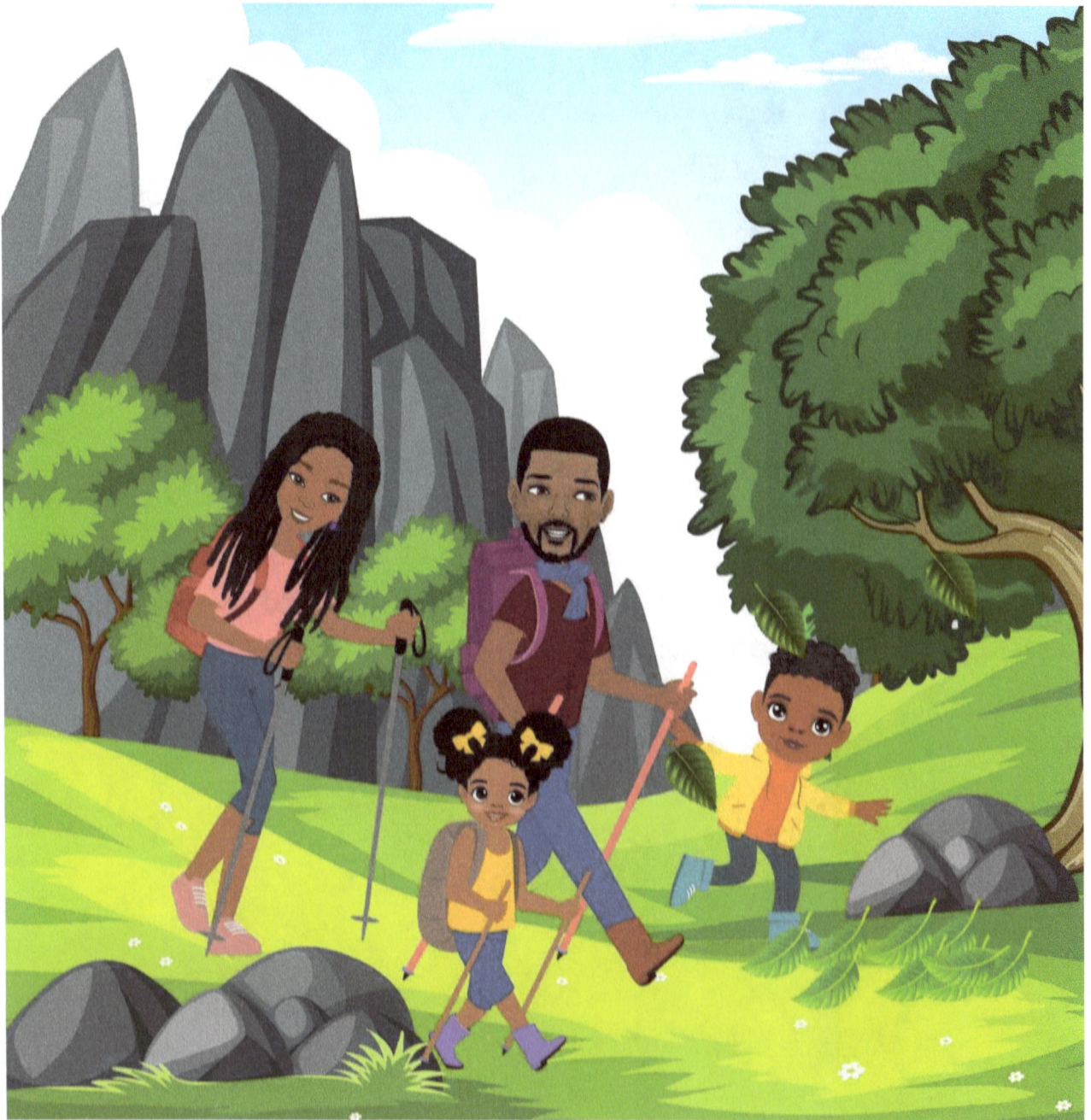

The heavens declare the glory . of God; the skies proclaim the work of his hands.

Day after day they pour forth speech; night after night they reveal knowledge. **Psalms 19:1-2**

For since the creation of the world God's invisible qualities—his eternal power and divine nature—have been clearly seen, being understood from what has been made, so that people are without excuse. **Romans 1:20**

Chapter 5
Hidden Wonders on the Trail

The sun peeked through the trees, casting dappled shadows on the forest floor. Noah was ready to explore the nature trail on the military base with his camcorder in hand. He loved being outdoors, surrounded by the sights and sounds of nature.

"Look, a deer trail!" he exclaimed, pointing to a narrow path winding through the trees. He zoomed in with his camcorder, recording the hoof prints in the soft earth. "I wonder if we'll see any deer today."

Dad pointed to a towering oak tree. "That's a mighty oak, Noah. See how its branches reach up to the sky?"

Noah tilted his head back, trying to see the top of the tree. "It's so tall! I bet it's been here for a long time."

Mom knelt and pointed to a patch of wildflowers. "Look at these beautiful colors! The bees and butterflies love these flowers."

Noah zoomed in on a butterfly fluttering from flower to flower. "It's like a tiny flying rainbow!"

He remembered how inferencing was like being a detective, using clues to solve problems. He scanned the forest floor for signs of animal life.

"Hmm," he pondered, "those acorns under the oak tree... I bet a squirrel buried them there!" He recorded his observation with the camcorder. "This could be evidence of squirrel activity!"

Dad pointed to a bird's nest nestled in the branches of a pine tree. "What kind of bird made that nest, Noah?"

Noah studied the nest, noticing the twigs and leaves woven together. "Maybe a robin?" he inferred.

"That's a good guess," Dad said. "Robins often build their nests in trees."

Mom encouraged Noah to listen to the sounds of the forest. "Can you hear the birds singing, Noah? They're communicating with each other."

Noah closed his eyes and listened to the symphony of chirps and tweets. He imagined the birds calling to each other, warning of danger or attracting a mate.

He thought about how all the living things in the forest were connected. The plants provided food and shelter for the animals, and the animals helped spread the plants' seeds.

"It's like a big puzzle," Noah said, "where everything fits together."

As they continued their hike, Mom opened her Bible and showed Noah Psalm 19:1-2: "The heavens declare the glory of God; the skies proclaim the work of his hands. Day after day, they pour forth speech; night after night, they reveal knowledge."

"The forest is telling us about God?" Noah asked.

Mom nodded. "Everything in nature points to God's power and creativity."

They also read Romans 1:20: "For since the creation of the world God's invisible qualities—his eternal power and divine nature—have been seen, being understood from what has been made, so that people are without excuse."

Noah looked around at the towering trees, the colorful wildflowers, and the busy insects. He realized that even the smallest creature was a part of God's unique creation. He felt a sense of wonder and gratitude for the beautiful world around him.

Activity:
Nature Journal

Objective: To observe and document nature, practice inferencing skills, and appreciate the interconnectedness of living things.

Materials:

- Noah's video camcorder
- Notebook and pencils or crayons
- Magnifying glass (optional)
- Bag for collecting leaves (optional)

Procedure:

1. **Explore the Trail:** Take a walk on a nature trail. Encourage Noah to observe the plants, animals, and insects.

2. **Record Observations:** Use the camcorder to document the different things you see. Have Noah narrate his observations and describe what he finds.

3. **Collect and Examine:** Collect leaves, rocks, or other natural objects (make sure they're allowed on the trail) and examine them closely with a magnifying glass.

4. **Draw and Describe:** Draw pictures of your observations in the nature journal. Write descriptions of the plants, animals, and their habitats.

5. Make Inferences: Encourage Noah to make inferences about the things he observes.

- "Why do you think that plant is growing in that location?"
- "What do you think that animal eats?"
- "How do the plants and animals depend on each other?"

6. Scripture Connection: Read Psalm 19:1-2 and Romans 1:20 together. Discuss how nature reveals God's glory and how we can learn about Him by observing His creation.

Tips for Parents:

Encourage Noah to use all his senses to explore the natural world.

Help him connect his observations to the science concepts of ecosystems, plant life, and animal tracks.

Discuss the importance of respecting and protecting the environment.

Enjoy the time spent together in nature and appreciate the beauty of God's creation.

Noah's Amazing Discoveries

Noah's Science Adventures: On the Trail of Amazing Discoveries followed the exciting explorations of a young, budding scientist named Noah! With his trusty camcorder by his side and his amazing family cheering him on, Noah uncovered the secrets of the world around him.

He started his journey by observing the fantastic teamwork of ants on the base playground, learning how they communicate and work together to achieve a common goal. Then, he turned his camcorder to the sky, capturing the dance of the clouds and learning how they bring rain to nourish the earth.

Noah transformed into a dinosaur detective at the museum, unearthing clues about these ancient creatures from their fossilized remains. He learned about their incredible size, their unique features, and the mystery of their extinction.

His adventures continued at the zoo, where he encountered fascinating animals from the African savanna. He observed their behaviors, learned about their adaptations, and discovered how they all play a vital role in the ecosystem.

Finally, Noah explored the wonders of a nature trail, discovering hidden signs of wildlife and learning how plants and animals depend on each other in a delicate balance. He realized that even the smallest creature is a part of God's unique creation.

Throughout his journey, Noah used his "inferencing" powers – like a detective using clues to solve a mystery – to understand the world around him. He learned that by observing carefully, asking questions, and seeking answers, he could unlock amazing discoveries about God's creation.

Noah's Science Adventures showed him that science is everywhere, from the tiniest ant to the giant dinosaur, from the clouds in the sky to the leaves on the trees. And most importantly, it showed him that every discovery is an opportunity to learn more about God's tremendous power and love.

Ways Parents Can Support Noah:

- **Encourage Curiosity:** Continue to answer Noah's questions and encourage him to explore with his camcorder.
- **Provide Opportunities:** Take advantage of the base resources and their memberships to museums and zoos.
- **Facilitate Exploration:** Allow him to explore the natural world and record his findings.
- **Model Inferencing:** Ask questions that prompt him to think critically about his observations.
- **Review and Discuss:** Watch Noah's videos together and discuss his observations and inferences.
- **Connect to Learning:** Relate his observations to books, videos, and other learning resources.

Additional Resources to Enhance Inferencing Skills:

At Home

Picture Books: Choose books with detailed illustrations and minimal text to encourage inferences about characters' feelings, motivations, and the story's setting.

Examples: "Where the Wild Things Are" by Maurice Sendak, "The Snowy Day" by Ezra Jack Keats, "Corduroy" by Don Freeman

Household Objects: Use everyday objects to spark inferential thinking.

"This spoon is wet. What can you infer about what just happened?"

"Look, the grass is wet. Why do you think that is?" (Possible inferences: it rained, the sprinklers were on)

"Kenlyn is crying. Why do you think she might be sad?" (Possible inferences: she fell, she wants a toy)

"Dad is putting on his uniform. Where do you think he might be going?" (Possible inferences: to work on the military base, to an exercise)

"Mom is putting on her coat and hat. What can you infer about the weather outside?" (Possible inferences: it's cold, it might be raining or snowing)

"The trash can is overflowing. What can you infer about what happened?"

Cooking: Baking and cooking provide excellent opportunities for making inferences.

Before Cooking:

"This recipe calls for lemons. What do you think they will add to our dish?" (Possible inferences: sourness, freshness)

"We need to chill the dough for an hour. Why do you think we need to do that?" (Possible inferences: to make it firmer, to slow down the yeast)

"Look at this picture in the cookbook. How do you think our dish will look when it's finished?" (Possible inferences: golden brown, bubbly, colorful)

During Cooking:

"The onions are starting to turn translucent. What do you think that means?" (Possible inferences: they are becoming softer; they are ready for the next ingredient)

"Listen to that sizzling sound! What do you think is happening to the food in the pan?" (Possible inferences: it's cooking, the heat is changing it)

"We're adding spices to the soup. How do you think the spices will change the flavor?" (Possible inferences: make it spicier, sweeter, more savory)

After Cooking:

"The bread rose so much in the oven! Why do you think that happened?" (Possible inferences: the yeast made it expand, the heat made it rise)

"The cookies are crispy on the outside and chewy on the inside. Why do you think they baked that way?" (Possible inferences: the baking time, the temperature, the ingredients)

"This dish smells delicious! What ingredients do you think we can taste?" (Possible inferences: garlic, herbs, lemon)

Nature in our Neighborhood: explore the natural world around home and community.

In the Yard:

"**Look at how tall the grass has grown! Why do you think it's so tall now?**" (Possible inferences: it rained a lot, it's been sunny, nobody has cut it)

"**The leaves on that tree are changing color. What season do you think it is?**" (Possible inferences: fall/autumn)

"**Those flowers are wilting. What do they need to perk up again?**" (Possible inferences: water, sunlight)

"**See that bird building a nest in that tree? Why do you think it chose that spot?**" (Possible inferences: it's safe from predators, it's close to food)

"**There's a spider web on the porch. What can you infer about the spider that built it?**" (Possible inferences: it's nearby, it eats insects that fly near the porch)

At the Playground:

"**The slide is hot! Why do you think that is?**" (Possible inferences: the sun has been shining on it)

"**The ground under the swings is bare. Why do you think there's no grass there?**" (Possible inferences: lots of people walk there, the swings block the sunlight)

"**Look at that pinecone on the ground. What can you infer about the trees in this park?**" (Possible inferences: there are pine trees nearby, maybe squirrels live here too)

"**Someone left their jacket on the bench. Why do you think they left it behind?**" (Possible inferences: they forgot it, they got too hot playing)

On the Nature Trail

Animal Tracks: Encourage observation and deduction.

"What kind of animal made these tracks? Big or small? How many toes?"

"Where do you think the animal was going? What might it have been doing?"

Bird Nests: Observe nests and infer about the birds that built them.

"What materials did the birds use to build this nest? Why do you think they chose those materials?"

"How many eggs are in the nest? What kind of birds do you think they belong to?"

Plant Life: Examine different plants and make inferences about their needs.

"Why do you think this plant is growing in the shade? What does that tell us about its needs?"

"This plant has thorns. Why do you think it has those?"

Weather: Observe the weather and make inferences about the environment.

"The ground is wet. What can you infer about the weather earlier today?"

"It's windy today. How do you think that will affect the animals and plants?"

Zoo

Animal Behavior: Observe animals and infer about their behaviors and needs.

"Why is the lion pacing back and forth? How is it feeling?"

"The monkeys are grooming each other. Why do you think they do that?"

Animal Habitats: Compare different habitats and infer how they meet the animals' needs.

"Why do you think the polar bear exhibit has a pool of cold water?"

"How is the desert exhibit different from the rainforest exhibit? How does that help the animals?"

Animal Adaptations: Examine animal features and infer their purpose.

"Why do you think the giraffe has such a long neck?"

"How does the tiger's stripes help it survive?"

Zookeeper Talks: Listen to zookeepers and make inferences about animal care and conservation.

"Why do the zookeepers feed the animals at specific times?"

"What can we do to help protect these animals in the wild?"

Museums

Historical Artifacts: Examine objects from the past and infer how they were used.

"What do you think this tool was used for? How do you know?"

"What can this object tell us about the people who lived long ago?"

Science Exhibits: Explore interactive exhibits and make inferences about scientific concepts.

"What happens when you press this button? Why do you think that happens?"

"How does this model help us understand the human body?"

Art: Observe artwork and infer the artist's message or the emotions being conveyed.

"What do you think the artist was trying to say with this painting?"

"How does this sculpture make you feel? Why do you think that is?"

Museum Guides: Listen to museum guides and make inferences about the exhibits and their significance.

"Why is this artifact considered so important?"

"What can we learn from this exhibit about our history or the world around us?"

Everyday Inferencing Questions

"Why do you think that person is smiling?"

"What do you think will happen if we leave the ice cream out in the sun?"

"Why is the car making that noise?"

"What do you think is in that package?"

"Why do you think the baby is crying?"

"What might happen if we don't water the plants?"

"Why do you think the dog is wagging its tail?"

"What can we learn from this story?"

Meet the Author of
Noah's Science Adventures:
On the Trail of Amazing Discoveries

Alisa Ladawn Grace, a retired school administrator, Chief Operating Officer of a nonprofit organization, and a Transformation Life Coach, is a dedicated advocate for empowering children through education. Her Specialist Degree in Curriculum and Instruction and her career-long commitment to creating impactful learning experiences for young minds underscore her expertise and dedication. Her extensive background in education, paired with her passion for teaching, has enabled her to develop engaging and informative content that supports children's academic and personal growth, ensuring the highest quality for her readers.

In her latest book, *Noah's Science Adventures: On the Trail of Amazing Discoveries*, Alisa taps into her love for exploration and learning to inspire children to dive into the world of science. This exciting adventure story introduces young readers to the wonders of science, encouraging curiosity and discovery. Alisa believes science is not just about facts—it's about asking questions, making discoveries, and developing a lifelong love for learning.

Alisa is also the author of the practical guide *Unlocking Your Great Potential Within You: The Supernatural Powers of Meditation, Executive Functioning Skills, and Good Habits for Kids 3-18 Years Old*. This guide is a comprehensive toolkit for success and well-being, equipping children with practical tools they can apply immediately. It emphasizes the importance of faith, integrity, and love in a practical and meaningful way for young minds, empowering them to take charge of their own growth and development and providing parents and educators with practical tools for their children's development.

Through her writing, Alisa seeks to make a lasting and positive difference in the lives of children and families, helping them grow not just academically but emotionally and spiritually as well. Her passion for education and unwavering commitment to fostering a love of learning are evident in her work, inspiring young readers to embark on their own journeys of discovery and unlocking the great potential within every child. Her dedication is sure to inspire and motivate her readers.

Join Noah on an Amazing Adventure!

Grab your explorer hat and get ready to discover the wonders of science in your own backyard! In Noah's science Adventures: On the Trail of Amazing Discoveries, you'll join a curious young scientist named Noah as he explores the world around him with his trusty video camcorder.

From observing busy ants on the playground to uncovering dinosaur secrets at the museum, Noah's adventures are filled with exciting discoveries and opportunities to learn about God's amazing creation. Along the way, he'll use his "inferencing" powers — like a detective using clues — to understand the mysteries of nature.

Get ready to:

Track amazing ant trails and learn about teamwork and communication.
Become a cloud detective and discover how weather patterns work.
Uncover dinosaur secrets hidden in ancient fossils.
Go on a wild safari at the zoo and meet incredible animals.
Explore nature trails and find hidden treasures in your own backyard.
Filled with fun facts, engaging activities, and inspiring Scripture connections, Noah's Science Adventures is the perfect book for budding scientists of all ages!